FAMILY ALBUM

FAMILY ALBUM

Sheree Mack

To: Morren
Lovely to meet you
Hope you enjoy
All the Best.
Sheree Mack
09/07/14
Brighton.

FlambardPress

First published in Great Britain in 2011 by Flambard Press
Holy Jesus Hospital, City Road, Newcastle upon Tyne NE1 2AS
www.flambardpress.co.uk

Typeset by BookType
Cover Design by Gainford Design Associates
Cover Art by Sheree Mack

Printed in Great Britain by Bell & Bain, Glasgow

A CIP catalogue record for this book is available from the British Library.

ISBN: 9781906601232

Flambard Press wishes to thank Arts Council England
for its financial support.

Supported by
ARTS COUNCIL
ENGLAND

Flambard Press is a member of Inpress.

The paper used for this book is FSC accredited.

to my son, Nathan,
with thanks for showing me the meaning
of compassion and generosity, everyday

Acknowledgements

Acknowledgements are due to the following: *Fabric, Interpoetry, Literary Review, Madeline, Nthposition, Other Poetry, Poui: The Cave Hill Literary Annual, Sable Litmag, Shadowlands, Ten by Ten, The Green Door, The New Writer, The Ranfurly Review, The Rialto.*

Some poems have appeared in the following anthologies: *Brown Eyes Anthology* (Matador, 2006), *Hair Anthology* (Suitcase Press, 2006), *Modern Love* (Crocus Press, 2007), *Sexual Attraction Revealed Anthology* (Anchor House Press, 2007).

A selection of these poems also appeared in the pamphlet *Like the Wind Over a Secret* (ID on Tyne Press, 2009).

The author received a Decibel and Arts Council England Spotlight Award 2003–2004.

The author received residences at The Literary and Philosophical Society, The North of England Institute of Mining and Mechanical Engineering; Can Serrat, Barcelona Spain; and MAS-SAMple, Caribbean Residences, Trinidad and Tobago and Barbados in 2007–2009.

Contents

'At this point, we can situate the family album somewhere between the genealogy and the saga, the first schematic and suggestive of a family tree, the second formulaic and embroidered with lore. Taking something from both, the family album amounts to an expression of identity.'

Martha Langford

tending to the past

after Etheridge Knight

there are people buried who are not content to rest in silence/
they haunt me/their words ripple upwards and outwards/
calling to me/calling me back
to those photo albums stacked neglected/
creased worn-torn soiled sepia and black and white/
images of generations/gone with the wind

i did not make it/it was already there waiting for me
voices calling me into the past/wanting me to knit their faces
together into some kind of whole/knitting isn't my strength/
once i drop a stitch a gap
is created/a gap   i try to fill with false memories

my great granddad/mother's mother's side/why did you come to england
you left the heart of darkness for this land, where your fire was soon put
      out/
i feel the texture of your suit/i recognise your straight back/the poser
      without/
your stance/but the details are fabrications

i did not name it/it was already there waiting for me
voices calling me back to the land of the hummingbird/
where i smell the fragrant air of immortelle/
see the emerald velvet hills touch the sky

my father/you left the crown colony
for this land/where your blood was poisoned/
i know your style with your hand in your left pocket/
the poser/no hint of a smile/a performer/the truth/
never known

i did not mould it/it was already there waiting for me
voices calling me into the past/wanting me to gather the
lost threads of experiences/
but my hands are shaky and awkward/the road map of lines
leads down deadends/roundabouts and detours/access denied

11

my great granddad/mother's father's side/
you left little england's sugar cane behind for this
land where you spread   your   seed   far   and   wide/
your woodcutter's hands/veins like ropes/thumbs flat and discoloured/
i know the grain of your skin/i sense the width of your nose/
the poser with a pigeon breast/your longevity a fact/the finer points a
    mystery

i am not sure what it should be/but it was here waiting for me
i rememory/i feel the intense heat/
i sleep with red ants/rise anew/
a different look in my eyes/a different look from my eyes

i know your style is mine/i know your blood is mine
remembering faces/names/dates and histories
is the task in hand to validate me/
but the   gaps   continue   to   grow as time passes by
but these photographs root me/stay/

i know your fabric/i feel your fabric in my blood
i am not sure what it should be/i know this is not my voice/
i know i did not make it/name it/mould it
but it was there waiting for me/i know you are mine

Why Did You Come to England?

Name: Charles Mason.
English, not the African name.

How can I know the real Great Granddad
without knowing your real name?

Why did you come to England?

What was so wrong with your life on the Gold Coast
that you had to leave all you knew for another world?

What was the beauty of England
except a word resting on the lips of a sailor?

Why did you come to England?

Looking at your face, with no hint of a smile,
was it worth the sacrifice?

You found a red-haired Geordie woman and
two children who you never saw reach double figures.

Why did you come to England?

The Stoker, 1915

I sit here with my back ramrod straight,
waiting for the man to fix his light-box.

I sit here with my suit and white white collar,
shoes shined, hair parted and ironed down straight.

I sit here now with my hat like a dome
perched on the small table beside me.

I sit here with memories of travelling
across the sea, away from my people.

I sit here with my back turned from my gods
as I followed the gentlemen with fire.

I sit here knowing I cannot return;
I have forsaken my father's name.

I sit here looking the viewer in the eye,
ever bold in my life choice, knowing Ma's proud.

I sit here with my back ramrod straight
in the belly of a ship like a gentleman.

Arrival, 1915

Spring, and you march through the streets; on corners,
green buds. Your step, light. What will the day bring?
Your thick lips still coated with a salty
residue. Hair-straightened material
like the compass needle pointing south. Specks
of white pin the sky. Sparks charge through your bones.

You stretch your limbs far and wide, creaking bones
after weeks of living in small corners,
cramped down low, noisy, tending flames, speckle
embers escape, singeing the skin, bringing
tears to your eyes. Here thoughts materialise;
waved to Ma until she was a speck of salt

in the distance. Pa, too proud to grind salt,
converse with the gods or scatter the white bones
to learn the fate in the material
world for his son. Like a caged wolf cornered,
he stayed in the hut. A merchant ship brought
you in time to England, a place speckled

with a few brown faces. New words speckle
the air from tunnel mouths as white as salt
and as sharp. In the town centre, bringing
your village ways with you, back stiff as bone,
stride confident, you stop at the corner.
There's a shop full of hats, materials

you could only dream of. Material,
a hat, makes a gentleman. Light speckles
off the store glass, your reflection cornered.
Your gaze held by a fine pillar of salt,
scarlet wild hair trying on a box-boned
bonnet, twirling in the mirror. This brings

smiles to your flawless face, a skipped beat brought
to your heart. Crushed rose skin. Material
of your bonnet should be silk, not stiff-boned,
but smooth. Your eyes, amber and gold speckles
catch, like sunset over the plains. Once more, salt
peppers your lips. You roll to love's corner.

White Women

Within my family there are white women.
White women who married black men. I forget,
neglect the fact, that their blood flows through mine.

Trace the past, a sea of faceless white is mine.
The black men forefront, a mist of women
behind. Their names I don't know or forget.

They are the enigma, shadows. Forget
the cleaning and cooking, their duty and mine,
they went against the grain, steadfast women.

In the corner of the frame, you white women
are not forgotten. Your spirit is mine.

Mahogany

The trees my great granddad grew,
on his own plot of land, he took an axe

and branch by branch,
he stripped the trees

and set to work,
with the grain, scraping,

creating smooth glossy limbs
ready to pattern for the British market.

Caressing Wood

Thomas Melgram, 1916

Large, dry-skinned, dusty hands.
Yellow, shortened nails,
flat fingers and rough palms.
The backs, a network of thick veins, like rope.
He runs his fingers across a chunk of wood.
His touch slow and deliberate.
Feeling the cool softness against his skin,
his eyes close briefly and his lips fall open
as he pulls in a slow, deep breath.
He rubs his fingertips over and over
the grain. A lethargic smile crosses his lips
as he spreads his fingers apart again.
The wood is talking and his hands are all ears.

In Bed With Hats

We ask . . .

What shall we do with
this stilted photograph
of our great granddad?

And why, when we see
him later, is he in a hospital
bed surrounded by family?

What about a wife?
He must have had one
or two, judging by their numbers.

Maybe she's in the corner
of the frame, the white
slender hand lost on the pillow?

Of course, there were his hats,
we can't forget them.
Nor would he wish us to.

Taking all his grooming skills
to place those growing larger hats,
by the year, on his shrinking head.

We're told . . .

he was an immigrant, a dresser,
opinionated. The war,
the club, the movement.

They got together
a year's engagement
of family squabbles.

Five years together and each one
saw a child until
one took her last breath.

The memory of his first wife
was maintained in the fullness
of affection for the second.

Worn out, thin and pale,
on the birth of the eighth child
taken again. Him, still alive.

But again the hats, grander,
his face never breaking a smile,
monkey-like, dignified.

We see . . .

him in bed, still
his family vivid, feeding
his ideas of grandeur.

Another hat, in a box,
a recent present, he never
got to wear in the open air.

Always deep sad eyes,
no grin. The look of
a man always alone,

looking for something that was there
all along – if only he could
see past his brim.

Easy Bones Café, 1940

At the flicks, he's cornered
in the back row. He brings
fellow soldiers, fresh from shovelling salt
into bags, feeling the grains still under their uniforms' material.
The film starts to roll, speckles
come to life on the screen. Already he's numb to the bone.

The usual stiff English accent talks over black-and-white visuals of
    boney,
fresh-faced soldiers marching in time, round the corner,
into the streets lined with cheering people. People throwing speckles
of coloured paper, praying that time will bring
their loved ones back, unharmed. It's immaterial
if they win or lose as lives are lost like wind carrying beads of salt.

He pictures himself in the marching lines. The salt
of anticipation coats his mouth as his bones
scream out for action, resenting the present squeeze of the velvet
    material
of his seat. His eyes rest on the right-hand corner
near the front. Her profile signals a beauty. Toasted freckles bring
pins and needles, starting at his toes, as desire speckles.

The film drones on, a distant speck
as his interest lies with her; cheeks salted
with rose, her ebony hair curled around her elegant neck, bringing
to Newcastle an Amazonian. Outside, waiting, he cups his boney
fingers around a Woodbine, inhaling deeply. She rounds the corner
on the arm of his brother, giggling, a sound like raindrops on taut
    material.

They talk briefly. She's aware of his smile, his khaki material
from head to toe. She holds on tighter to her beau's arm and speckles
their conversation with hushed words, all the time watching from the
      corner
of her eye the brother, with the Woodbine and that smile. A smile as
      sharp as salt
unexpected on the tongue. Having coffee and toast at the Easy Bones
Café, she stares into her cup thinking what a night with him would
      bring.

The slow easy smile from the corners of his mouth up to his caramel
      eyes brings
a lightness to her head. Already having one man is immaterial;
this brother is different. His smile speaks to her young bones
and makes her reckless. She forgets her fine training as sin speckles
her cinnamon frame. To go with him would be adding salt
to the wounds. The next night, they meet at six on the corner.

Waiting

Tommy Melgram Jr

There's a photograph of him
standing on Newburn's High Street,
trees in cherry-blossom full,
hands in the pockets of his best suit,
as his eyes look beyond this scene.

He waits for her to come
out from her mam's house behind.
He's been to war and sailed the seas,
but she remembers the nights since
that he's been out all night.

'I've been to me friend's –
Ah got too drunk.'
She's like a pawnshop –
takes owt in.
But she remembers everything.

Sweetie

It is shaped like
a rugby ball
but lime green.

Taking off the sticky paper
reminds me of
hot spitting coals.

Once in my mouth,
still tasting of Cellophane.
It's a soft shell around a hard core.

Bullets.
That's what Nana used to call them,
bullets.

She'd have a stash of them in her handbag.
I'd be passing out with travel sickness
before she'd part with one.

'Make it last,' she'd say,
popping another in her mouth
and adjusting her wig in one swift movement.

Not a Fighting Chance

Now that he cannot walk,
now that he sits, unmoving,
calliper on abscessed knee, supported
in the recliner armchair, positioned below
the sitting-room window, I forget the one
who at the age of fourteen
boxed his way through West Yorkshire
to feed and clothe his siblings.
Once he enters the last hospital ward,
I forget the man who
tangoed around the women
in order to dance into the boxing ring,
all attention focused on his opponent.
I've long forgotten his lethal left jab
and his fierce uppercut.
It's as if the fight has abandoned
this ugly ogre nursing a swollen stomach,
belching up black bile into a glass dish.
He has left behind forever that young man,
that high-polished caramel man, my granddad,
that keen-storytelling man. And long before
I knew him, that man who could only run
for miles, or fight for title or country.
A frog who stares with bulging eyes,
the way he lies there, now, with his eyes open,
for a moment with the dignity of an African President.
I stay beside him, like his corner man at ringside,
ducking and diving in unison but not sharing his pain.
His limbs, grained like marble, glisten
in the spotlights.

Port of Spain, Trinidad

The woman's skirt is the map of the town;
along the hem runs the blue blue sea,
a constant pull onto the port,
where the silk cotton trees crowd.

Look close at the intricate detail,
like the flipped-off lid of an inkwell,
splattered black lines run deep and wide,
dividing up this vibrant masterpiece.

Just off centre is Laventille, where
metal roof hovels crouch like crabs
in the hills. Tempers brew, sparks
fizz from the overhead electric cables.

Harsh showers send sewers and earth
swimming along the old streets,
tunnelling and burrowing
looking for home.

Mother/Mother Country

Years of it, years of it, burning, burning
to feel your arms open and pull him in,
to feel you smile up to your eyes with pride,
to feel you, meet him, like the sea flowing.

Years of it, years of it, burning, burning,
land he bought with money he put aside,
built a house with veranda alongside,
to feel you meet him like the sea flowing.

Years of it, years of it, burning, burning,
to the other children your tongue was sweet,
to him, outside child, the leather would smart,
to feel you meet him like the sea flowing.

Years of it, years of it, burning, burning,
he took his suit and grip and stowed away
on the big ship to the other mother,
to feel her meet him like the sea flowing.

Years of it, years of it, burning, burning
now, you cry for the son you had and lost,
waiting for him to come back home to touch,
to feel him, meet you, like the sea flowing.

His Possessions

a suitcase
gold tooth
fur hat
wives

a passport blue
yellow palms
shoe horn
leukaemia

a quarter of pear drops
gramophone
mother back home
rage

When George Met Anita, March 1968

To the Black Diamond nightclub on the corner
of Manchester Road and Croft Street, you bring
a silent predatory style to salt
this razor-sharp scene. In your smooth blue suit, gabardine material,
after a short evening shower, slightly speckled,
charm your sinewy bones.

To the Black Diamond nightclub, with bones
jangling, you come with a friend. Hugging the corner,
you rearrange your full pink skirt, shot through with speckles
of silver thread. You bring
a certain kind of freshness to the material
of this place; a quality that irritates other women like grains of salt.

The Black Diamond nightclub isn't worth salt;
around for years, with its chipped tables and bony
stools. Pulling in punters with thumping bass and seamless vibes,
    material
heard nowhere else by the Coloured crowd. Entwining bodies in
    corners,
accepting what small pleasures it brings,
the spinning glass ball throws out lights in speckles.

Across the darkened room, you see each other, speckles
of light fizzing like stars in the cool night sky. Salty
beads of anticipation coat your top lip, bringing
goose-bumps to your flesh and a weakness to the bone.
You look again, out the corner
of your eye, longer this time, experiencing the feel of material.

Just as buds are blossoming, this is movie material.
It's love at first sight, not on the grey-speckled
screen, but playing out in real life, in a small corner
of this city, which built its wealth on salt
mines, deep white seams like bones.
You move from your side of the room, not sure what this will bring.

To the Black Diamond nightclub, you bring
no expectations, as they are immaterial,
but tonight as you two talk, the core of your bones
sing. In a short time, you write letters, speckles
of confetti as white as salt,
as your heart, once a cage in search of a bird, is cornered.

Wedding Day, 14 September 1968

The camera has caught them
in front of the swinging doors
of the registrar's office.

His stance is relaxed,
in a smart dark suit, leaning,
hand in pocket, casual.

His ebony skin smooth,
smiling broad white
concealing his vast years.

She clutches his cupped arm
staring straight into the lens.
No hint of a smile, serious.

Triangle glasses obscure
her high-cheek-boned face –
a blossoming beauty.

He's bedded many women.
Children, he has a few.
She leaves her village today.

In the humid space beneath
her turquoise two-piece,
her virginal body buckles.

She must step out of youth,
be his woman,
and keep her man happy.

Her nipple-less breasts
and sagging stomach
will have to yield to him.

Just the two of them,
her witch's spectacles off,
she pulls him into her side.

Bonny Baby Contest

In the stuffy old village hall,
in a corner, jam-packed
under the stairs, are Geordie
mothers smiling into the faces
of their babies for the camera.
My mum fixes the camera with
a weary stare.

Twenty-eight years old
and newly married,
my sister sits on her knee,
with head turned around,
making sure Mum's still
there. The touch of her knee
and hands not being enough.

Mum does not smile.
In Mum's face, I see my sister
grown, and in my sister's face
I see her son grown.
Between their years
and their stories,
time is running by.

Inventing Daddy in Bradford

If I could see nothing but the smoke
from the tip of his cigar, I would know
everything about his Windrush years.

If his spirit was contorted by the cold,
with the grey evening light, I would know
the rabbit-warren streets of back-to-back
terraces and broken-down backyards
were where he was allowed to live.

If I could see but his hands,
I could recognise their dexterity
as they would have played construction,
with spiral shafts and threshing
rotors, parts for a combined harvester.

I could reconstruct his strong jaw
and his hooded eyes that scared me,
but captivated the women back
to his room, keeping his bones
warm against the cold north wind.

With the damp cigar between his teeth,
I could know why he chose to forget
his home, put down roots here,
senses accommodating to the greasy
factory floors and screeching cogs.

If I could trace the two veins that bulged
across his temple when he was vex,
I would know of the passion that drove him
to this godforsaken country. But, if I had my way,
I would keep him far from Bradford
– like the come-hither tip of his cigar.

Growing Tomatoes in the Back Room

They hang in bunches
on vines, cheek to cheek,
each an orb of luminosity,

barred with claret bands
which scale the skins'
radiant segments,

like glistening rubies
in a jeweller's window.
Shimmering, solid

globes: think baubles,
a whizzing cricket ball,
blushing plump ladies,

think sun on horizon.
Glowing, and glowing,
and not one in any way

distinct from the other,
nothing about them
of individuality. Each

a perfect fulfilment
of precision. Your
handywork,

you who tends them
in the hot back room which
breathes in the day's heat.

You are relaxed here
tending a piece
of your island at home.

Pomegranate

There is a fullness about her,
her bosoms, the fold of her dress,
the contour of her shape downwards.
She's a glossy, rounded, wide fruit,
with a tough, leathery, neat skin.
She's a high yellow, heavily
overlaid with deep pink. Inside
is separated by membranous
walls, white spongy, bitter tissue,
divided into compartments,
packed with sacs filled with sweet juicy,
red, pink pulp. And in each sac is
one angular, soft, not hard, seed.

Seasoned in September, this seed
matures, but come January,
it is ripe. Cracks appear
on her thick rind. Watchful waiting.
High temperature is usually
essential for growth but this time
hampers development. Before
full-term, the precious garnet juice
runs away, wasted. There's sickly
skin, silver on the ward's stone floor.
This one will be retained in stained
memory. One that could have been.

Daddy

You as a child,
tall for your age, neat hair.
All elbows and knees,
rough-rounded joints.

You in chattel,
a circle of dirt as yard.
Heavy rains that pound
on the steel roof.

You crying,
hollow echo like drum.
Because you answered back,
because you asked why.

The mark of the devil
from repeated beatings.

Me as a child,
Afro like a halo.
Big soft rolls of flesh,
rough and scuffed knees.

Me in a flat
a concrete veranda with
pebble-dashed walls
for idle pickings.

Me crying,
wails of pain pierce our home.
Because I answered back,
because I asked why.

Weals of swelling skin
from repeated beatings.

Naughty Amelia Jane

She was a big white doll
with thick black curls
and rosy red cheeks.
She was looking sweet
in a white-and-pink frilly dress,
with white ankle socks
and black shiny shoes.

She was hated by the other toys;
the sailor, the golliwog
and the wind-up mouse.
They tried to keep out of her way
as she liked to push them off the shelf
on to the floor, to get them dirty.
She always wanted to be the favourite.

He'd read all about her at bedtime.
He'd sit on the edge of my bed,
soften his eyes and his voice,
and read chapters, just for me.
This was the only time he was close.
The only time I could ask questions.
The only time I felt loved, by him.

Three-Legged Stool

Three screws used to nip my flesh like pincers.
I focused on the wallpaper; cream tiles
with bowls of oranges and apples, and jugs.

Jugs, I imagined held milk, warmed,
creamy and sweet; no clinging skin on top
but gushing freely like a geyser.

I couldn't eat the mash-up lamb, dumpling and rice.
She tried her best to eat hers and mine.
He was in before I could hide. I was

damn farce. As a boy he never had such food.
His rage ricocheted in our cramped
kitchen. The stool chalked the floor

as he pulled me off.
His large yellow-palmed hand
sliced into my fleshy legs.

I focused on the polished wallpaper
with the waxy fruit and heavy jugs, still feeling the nip
of the three-legged stool, knocked onto the hard cold floor.

Takes a Firm Hand

He'll crack an egg firmly on the side of the bowl,
letting the yolk fall through the jagged edges
to land in the hollow made in the pile of flour and mix.
Pouring in milk from the glass bottle
onto large handfuls of juicy sultanas.

All the time, he'll be speaking over his shoulder to his wife,
who wonders how she'll cope once he's gone.
He sees his children looking through the sitting room hatch –
holds their gaze – 'Mind your Mother.'
Making sure the message hits home with his yellowing eyes.

He'll take a generous knob of butter and rub around and around
the flat tray, making sure that no corner is left untouched.
And then he'll pour a stream of slow-moving
mixture into the tray, not one creamy drop
escaping to stain his clean white kitchen bench.

I Have Learned To Be What I Am Not

It was 1977, silver jubilee, we were a family of four not five.
They wouldn't have had to try again if I had been
what they said I was, when I was born.

'It's a boy,' Nana rang Dad to tell him.
He cracked open the port and drew deeply on a cigar,
savouring the moment of finally fathering a son,
in England, after so many, many girls.

I have learned to be what I am not.

I watched Saturday, all day, *World of Sport*, jockeying
my horse past the finishing post, pinning my opponent down
on the canvas and challenging him when he told me to do
as I was told and sit still.

I took his vexness, like any son, on the chin with attitude,
so I didn't have to feel the breath that betrayed the sense of
disappointment.

I have learned to be what I am not.

To keep the little six-year-old girl with bunnies and buck teeth
hidden away under the bedroom table with her ballerina
Sindy Doll.

Bunk Beds

There's movement above as she rolls and moans.
The slates rattle. I lie on my back.
A finger doodles on her mattress
and my mind creates the colours.
Through the double glazing, inside,
are the muffled sounds of traffic
and the distant rubble of his snores.

I breathe shallow breaths,
as the layers of itchy blankets weigh
Bunnie and me down.
My body, in high-collar nightie, burns.
I do not move. Shiny pine bars
frame my dreams,
frame my warm damp pool.

Daddy Lion

It is dark when we reach the hospital,
after the journey of
diesel mixed with cramped bodies.
The place looms large with
only small windows of light.
We go through the swing doors
into floors, walls and benches all
white upon harsh white.

Along a stretched corridor,
I look for
the Snow Queen and her sleigh.
I only meet men
in white coats.

Somewhere up high
we enter a side room.
The curtains are drawn.
He is there
bathed in spotlight.
The beast of my life
is tied to the bed by sheets.
His head is shaved.

At Mum's touch his eyes open.
His heavy pupils swim in a yellow sea.
She kisses his hollow cheek.
His lips barely move.
His roar is a moan.
His claws are broken.
His chest is cold.

Coup d'État

I can picture him
at the bathroom mirror
clipping his close-knit Afro,
patting it down, trying to see
his handywork from all angles.

Or him on an evening
ready for the bookies,
resting his trilby hat, just so,
as if it would fall off,
but it doesn't.

If I listen carefully
I can hear him on the stairs:
'Can it be that life was so simple then,'
Roberta Flack style;
Or calling down to Eugene from the islands.

If I sniff the air
I can catch a whiff of Old Spice
after Sunday chicken and rice.
Then the odour of iodine
disturbs our home.

The leukaemia is in remission,
taking a rest before the *coup d'état*.
I can touch him, loose blue-black flesh
like thick treacle poured.
I hold his hand.

Oil and Steel

After Henri Cole

My dad lived in a run-down maisonette
watching a *Rediffusion* colour TV,
reading the Bible and pornographic
magazines, which he preferred to
company and *The Watch Tower*.

One by one the men from the islands
died of loneliness, except Eugene,
who was there to lay him out and,
holding a shot of one hundred percent white rum,
said, 'Now yuh home, at lang last.'

I took the feather from his hat
and a silk shirt from his wardrobe
as my inheritance.
I once saw him bawling like a baby
when he got a letter from back home.

After twenty-five years of silence, this man
who never showed much affection
buried his head on his wife's bosom.

Idol

Like the Egyptians worshipped the sun,
you were my sun.
I worked hard to make sure your rays fell on me.
With my ABCs on our home-made blackboard,
I was better than she,
yet she still held your sparks.
I stepped into your beams.
Solar maximum as I became the lioness
you, as the ringmaster, had to tame.

Like the orbit of an object
around its focus, under its influence,
my path was fixed. I absorbed your heat
and threw it back hard.
Increasing the friction
developing an atmosphere.
From the frequent
drags of sickness, you were losing energy.
Once your force was gone, I spiralled into
the black hole you left behind.

My Dad's Hat

Saturday mornings, while standing
on the bottom step, I would reach
up high to the hook in the passage,
tiptoeing to reach higher,
touching, and fumbling
the soft crown. I would imagine
it was a wild animal with soft warm fur,
asleep and purring.
A dusty wind hummed through
the fur and sent up a musky scent,
his scent I loved, lingering on the
band, the feather and the inner satin.
Here I would smell the bay rum
from his hair and I could almost think
I was being held, or walking by the water,
or touching the immortelle flame flowers,
blooms whose scent was that of caramelised
wood in the air, as now,
as I think of his final sleep.
I stand on this soft warm soil
and watch light slowly close
on the ripples of petals on the pond.

The Grip

We proceed backwards into the light
carrying it with us, his grip.

A brown battered leather suitcase
Oblong with cream creases along the joins.

Two round, rusty push-along locks
spring open, tooth-like catches.

Inside a rich silky smooth sage lining
with a small cream-leaf detail.

He could have come over in 1952
or '53 or '54. We don't know for sure.

He was a stowaway; him and his friend.
His silences held longings and shames.

Leaving the pain of the past behind caused a splitting
in the self that broke out in acts of violence.

To move forward, certain words, conversations,
had to evaporate from his lips.

Or hide in a narrow part of his brain.
I think he packed them away, away in his grip.

Then, he pushed the grip under the bed and forgot.
Never to be opened again in his lifetime.

Summer

Because it reminds me of safety,
I love the smell of milk-chocolate biscuits
from holidays in caravans at Newbiggin-by-the-Sea.
Because it reminds me of safety,
my heart remembers
my mum calling me in for a cup of hot sweet tea
when the rain hammered on the tin roof like tiny fists.
Because it reminds me of safety,
I love the smell of milk-chocolate biscuits
                              in summer showers.

Good Times

After Lucille Clifton

Mama's paid the rent
and the gasman
and the electric man
and the light is back on
and the front-room fire is glowing
and there's singing in the front room
and these be good times
children
good times
good times

no more postponed groceries
Mama's filled the pantry
and the fridge be full
with onions, tomatoes and ham
and the table be full
with apples, bananas and grapes
and there's dancing in the kitchen
and these be good times
good times
good times

oh children
think about the good times

Rollers

She took her time to tame her mass of hair.
First, she'd make a strong mug of tea and sit
at the high teak table with a plastic bag.
Her cigarette smoke would claim the air.

A long wide comb in a cup of water,
she'd pull it out, tapping off loose droplets,
before running the comb through her thin hair.
The comb would straighten out the grey-black frizz.

Still holding the sections, comb back in the cup,
she'd take a pink roller out of the bag
and start at the tips of her hair, rolling
upwards and under.

Only a pink-and-black sausage roll
was left in her hand ready for a grip,
like a white overcoat, encasing the roll.
She'd take a sip of tea and a quick drag.

Then she'd take the comb again, wet and pull
on her tangled locks until it was straight.
Rollers would be rolled up and under
and covers in place, again and again,

until her whole head was a mass of rows.
Pink and white rolls, like gums and teeth,
gradually drying, gradually curling
straight. After Sunday dinner and dishes done,

the rollers would be pulled out swiftly.
These relaxed curls were then teased out like notes
from a saxophone, until they danced around
her head like a lion's mane but tamed.

Ode to My Mum's Broth

Listen,
no one makes broth like my mum's,
with its chopped turnips
diced potatoes
and flakes of carrot;
a melody of colours.

Listen
to the touch of her pinny rustling
like the wind over a secret
as she moves from the bench to the stove
folding in the smooth butter beans
the translucent onions and pearl-soft barley.

Listen
to the broth thickening
as the gas hisses
and she seasons the
soup, the heart of the soup,
with her smile.

Listen,
no one makes broth like my mum's,
and I tell her and she
takes her eyes off the pot to smile
that smile, that is warmer
than the broth could ever be.

Listen,
I will need to taste this broth
in years to come,
scadding-hot broth, to warm my heart
when I'm away from home,
when she's away for good.

Ovaries

A snake has two; one in front of another.
Yours nestled, just below your 'floppy' tubes,
hanging, one each side of your womb;
the home, at one time or another,
for two children and a half.

Two walnut-shaped sacs,
pearl-coloured, hiding treasures
like a petulant teenager, but
bouncy and squishy
like putty stress balls.

Seeking medical advice about
the erratic nature of your monthlies,
at the age of fifty-seven, the consultant said
you had the ovaries of a seventeen year old.
Remarkable.

Did you feel the need ever
to reach in, clutch them? Lovingly
roll them between your fingers
slowly like hard-boiled eggs
without the shells?

It would just be your way
of making them feel needed,
making them feel wanted and alive.
They were aching for that something
they hadn't stumbled upon in a long time,

as you only had one love.
He was all the man you ever wanted.

Swan Song

It is a last-minute, beg, borrow or steal flight deal.
Her long-dead husband's sister invites her for a month.
She flies out the next week to Las Vegas,
loses her luggage en route, arriving into the hot, dry state
with one pair of clean knickers
and no blood-pressure tablets.

A shopping spree is needed
along with some late nights on the strip.
She's punching dimes into the one-armed bandits
and throwing chips across the green velvet tables,
hearing ice clink against the glass
as she savours another brandy and Babycham.

No one hears from her in a week.
They call the house, the other house,
the sister, the other sister.
Thoughts cross their mind of a hospital,
a car accident, off the dusty, windy track,
after a late-night drinking session in a saloon,
bearing in mind, she has no licence.

After seven days, she gets back in touch, calls
to say that she just popped down to Mexico.
They imagine her chauffeured across the border,
sombrero protecting her delicate pinky-beige scalp,
sporting a white T-shirt with '*Amo México*'
splayed across her ample chest.

Her arms are waving above her head
and her head is back, way back,
eyes closed, feeling the sun on her face
and her mouth is wide open as she laughs
as she's never laughed before, abandoning
herself to the moment.

Pig's Trotters

When I get to the house, I rush up the stairs,
doors swinging behind me.
I dive into the bedroom, zigzagging through bodies
to crash to the floor next to Mum's side. My sister,
still in her pyjamas, tells me Mum collapsed, then,
ten minutes later, she's salivating and babbling about 'the kids'.

I dash to the window, pulling back the gardenia curtains,
willing the ambulance to speed up,
I race back to her side, with the choking smell of urine,
straightening her cotton nightie,
smoothing her coarse hair. She's clutching her wedding rings.
I stroke her hands – cold hands.

I run back to the window, feel my airways tighten. I, who
have put on last night's clothes back to front, and I whisper,
Please hurry, steaming the pane. I catch the sirens,
muffled as they lumber up the hill. I glimpse two green men
jump out of flapping doors with a metal stretcher banging
off their thighs, taking the steps like an escalator,

then I take a deep breath, and I think,
take my heart, I will gladly give it
to have Mum off this floor and cuddling me again.
I've seen pictures of wailing women
over the bodies of their children, locked in that grief
like a vice. I long for such release.

Like men possessed, they feel her pulse,
press her chest, pump oxygen, release the bed
roll her on, tighten her in,
one two three, lift her up and out.
I walk down the path with my mum.
The air is heavy with dew; the clouds are

full and peaching. I breathe
as people breathe when they are trapped
underground, in gasps.
We lift up gently and do not stop until we reach the hospital.
I walk into that room and watch her feet,
dry and hard skinned, I cover them.

Sunday Meat

I take the meat out of the oven;
her Pyrex dish with a chod of beef,
forgotten for a week,
all shrivelled and dry,
lodged in a solid sea of fat.

I grieve for her now as I've never grieved before.
She was spicy, full-bodied port.

The only image that comes to mind
when I tap into my memory chest
is a shell on the hospital bed;
an old woman with a slur, dazed,
trapped in a sea of congealed fat.

I'm Becoming My Mum

After Lorna Goodison

red/brown woman
solid smile curtained
a stirring brew

my mum weaved reds,
yellows, purple strands of time, cuddles
and words to create a home with

potato hotpot from leftover Sunday roast to
cups of Bovril after *Coronation Street* but
before bedtime

my mum had a white cotton
nightie dotted with petit rose buds
it clung to her size

I have it now
it bellows like a pelican's bill
that would swallow the moon

I wear it now
feel the fabric touch my skin
like soothing calamine

red/brown woman
solid smile curtained
a stirring brew

Eyes Down, Look In

We are sitting, me and Sharon, in a
four-man booth. The packed bingo hall, waiting
for the main session to begin. Eyes down,
look in – when Mum comes in, after six months
dead. She takes an empty seat, clicks off her
markers and gets ready for prize bingo,
before and between the big-money game.

We are sitting in the no-smoking section.
Mum lights up and takes a deep draw, she smiles.
She's pleased with her full head of hair, rollered
into place around her pink-beige plump face.
'Three and six, thirty-six.' The caller starts.
Chatting is a no-no in any game,
but Mum's got a lifetime of things to say.

'Stop all the crying, Sharon. You'll make
yourself sick. Mick's shoulder can only take so
much. You know you're the strength in that coupling.'
Her chastisement a change. No one seems to
notice our table. Eyes down, silently
praying that their number will be out next.
'Nine and zero, top of the shop, blind ninety.'

Mum's fingers dance across the numbers, clink,
a comforting sound in the close, heavy air.
'Sheree, I'm working with you.' Her eyes never
leave her board. 'Hold on, you're not alone.
I'm working to bring happiness into
your life. But you've got to let the hurt out.'
Like coloured balls bubbling in the machine,

my grief bursts out in rounded orbs of pain.
I want to scream: you left us alone
to cope, to cope alone. My fantasies
of the prodigal daughter's return with
babe in arms were dashed as you slipped away
during the night. 'One and four, fourteen.' 'House.'
Mum groans as if her life depended on

that win. She starts to line up her thick red-
and-blue dabbers. Not green, as green's unlucky.
Even in death, she's still holding out for
that big win. Not wanting to see her hopes
dashed. Not wanting to see her leaving us
again, I look away through the sea of
cigarette smoke, and half-empty glasses.

Now

Smell of coconut milk,
plantain from the oven,
early morning haze,
penetrating.

Breathing as one,
the coppery-coloured couple
arms entwined,
their child within.

Rounded, smooth and warm
to the touch.
Naked
like porcelain.

Midnight jazz
with a hint of cinnamon.
Nutmeg vanilla.
Lingering.

Out On the Town

The plan is turn a different corner,
out of necessity. Decide bringing
myself, only. No more shedding salted
tears like my life is the material
of some crap soap opera, with speckles
of drama at Christmas. No more cold bones.

Out with the girls, shivering to the bone
in skimpy dresses, ready. On corners,
men show off muscles in white T-shirts, specks
of blood already from fighting. It brings
proof of their alpha-male material.
I'm no seasoned pro, just lightly salted.

At eleven, Flynn's throws us out like salt
onto slippery roads. We stagger bone-
to-bone to a club, dive material;
feet stick to the floor and shady corners.
Sucking cheap cocktails through bendy straws brings
an instant hit, all glitter and speckles.

Clutching our drinks, we walk the boards, speckles
of chat. I bump into him. He's salty,
says he's been gipped out of a tenner. 'Bring
out the management.' Pale blue, like old bone,
eyes connect with mine. He smiles. I'm cornered,
but no management materialise.

On the dancefloor, comic material.
He's moving to his own beat, limbs speckled
with sweat. I watch him from a dark corner.
He's Grizzly Adams, shaggy beard salted
with white. I take to the floor, shaking bones,
style and rhythm, showing what I could bring

to the party. The night wears late and brings
dawn. No more potential material,
until Pale Blue mashes into my bones.
No friends. Wallet empty. His plea speckled
with fluttering lashes, loaded with salt.
We roll to a taxi on the corner.

Termination

I didn't make that appointment.
That Sunday, I lay on the leather suite
in a foetal curl, crying like a baby.

Reel upon reel of images;
flowers, mourners, paparazzi,
photographs of the scene.

That repeated image of her in that
Royal-blue suit and high white collar,
shyly showing her engagement ring.

That image appeared on mugs and T-shirts.
Ding-dong, the people's princess is dead.
The voice-over said,

'The most precious gift of all is life.'

I didn't keep that appointment.

'You'll Never Be Lonely Again'

'It's the closest a woman comes to death.'
Electric ripples along the spine, legs akimbo; only visual
two peaks, knees. Head like a rag doll, floppy and damp,
seething pain, the belly like a drum.

A truth drug, the urge to push,
to rip flesh like bread. A grey, skinned
rabbit with an old man's face appears.
A slap, a cry, a life.

Live images fed on a reel over and over.
In the traffic-light strobes, his arms propel, windmill style.
Bareback, no street lights, no seatbelt rider
dives into the tunnel; later a missed-period.

Feet like puddings, carrying heavy load,
trip over stack of well-thumbed,
size of a fist at x weeks, breastfeeding baby books,
even the best-laid plans, ain't happening, to me. To me.

The air shoves its long arm down
my throat and pushes out, 'Mama.'

With a Veranda

Somehow, you've travelled thousands of miles
and years to stand in this cane field,
on the bumpy ridge, at the edge of the cliff;
not amongst the cocoa trees
but under the green honey creepers – you can
hear but not see them.
This is where your house will be, with a veranda
looking out, over the rolling sea.
Here, your mouth and your eyes are still,
all lines relaxed.
Your salt-and-pepper locks hang down,
gracing your mature frame.
The smell of gardenias, once sweet,
reminding you of the empty dinette
when your mum had left for the Club,
now smells sickly, as you take
a deep breath and your humped belly
pushes against your tightening red dress.